GRAPHIC SCIENCE AND ENGINEERING IN ACTION

THE **AMAZING STORY** OF

MOBILE PHONE TECHNOLOGY

MAX AXIOM
SUPER SCIENTIST

by Tammy Enz

illustrated by Pop Art Properties

Raintree

Raintree is an imprint of Capstone Global Library Limited,
a company incorporated in England and Wales having its registered office at
7 Pilgrim Street, London, EC4V 6LB – Registered company number: 6695582

www.raintreepublishers.co.uk
myorders@raintreepublishers.co.uk

Edited by Christopher L. Harbo and James Benefield
Designed by Ted Williams
Cover art by Marcelo Baez
Originated by Capstone Global Library Ltd
Production by Helen McCreath
Printed and bound in China

ISBN 978 1 4062 7970 2
18 17 16 15 14
10 9 8 7 6 5 4 3 2 1

British Library Cataloguing in Publication Data
A full catalogue record for this book is available from the British Library.

We would like to thank Akbar M. Sayeed at the University of Wisconsin
(Madison), USA, for his invaluable help in the preparation of this book.

All the internet addresses (URLs) given in this book were valid at the time
of going to press. However, due to the dynamic nature of the internet, some
addresses may have changed, or sites may have changed or ceased to exist since
publication. While the author and publisher regret any inconvenience this may
cause readers, no responsibility for any such changes can be accepted by
either the author or the publisher.

TABLE OF CONTENTS

A DYNAMIC DEVICE

A visit to the Grand Canyon sparks an investigation into mobile phone technology for Max Axiom, Super Scientist.

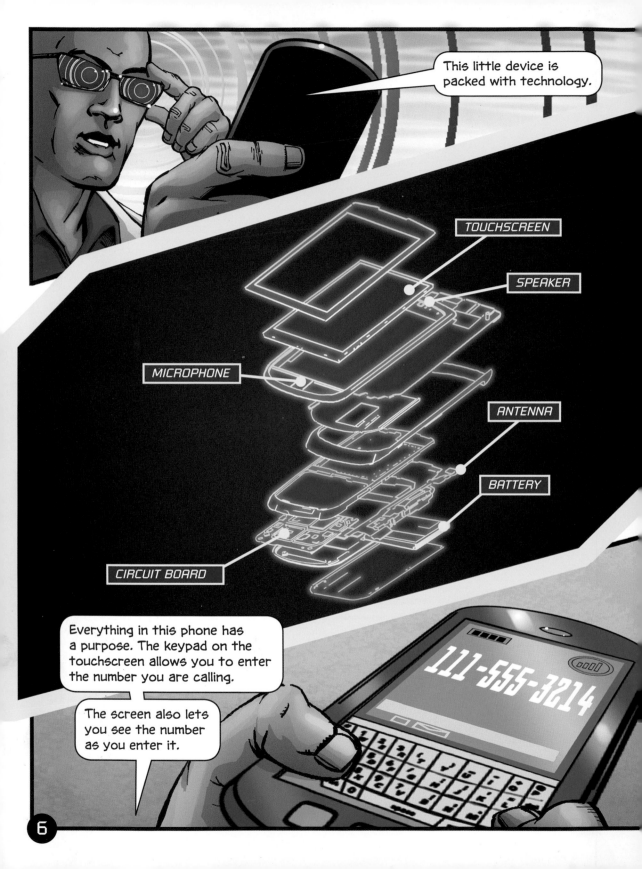

The microphone captures your voice to send it to the person you're calling.

The speaker projects the voice of the person you are talking with.

This tiny battery powers your phone for days.

And this circuit board is actually a very powerful computer.

But the antenna inside the mobile phone is especially important. It receives and sends radio waves.

BATTERIES

Mobile phones need a long-lasting, small battery to be useful for everyday life. Lithium-ion battery technology provides the needed power. Without this technology, batteries would only last a short time, making phones impractical.

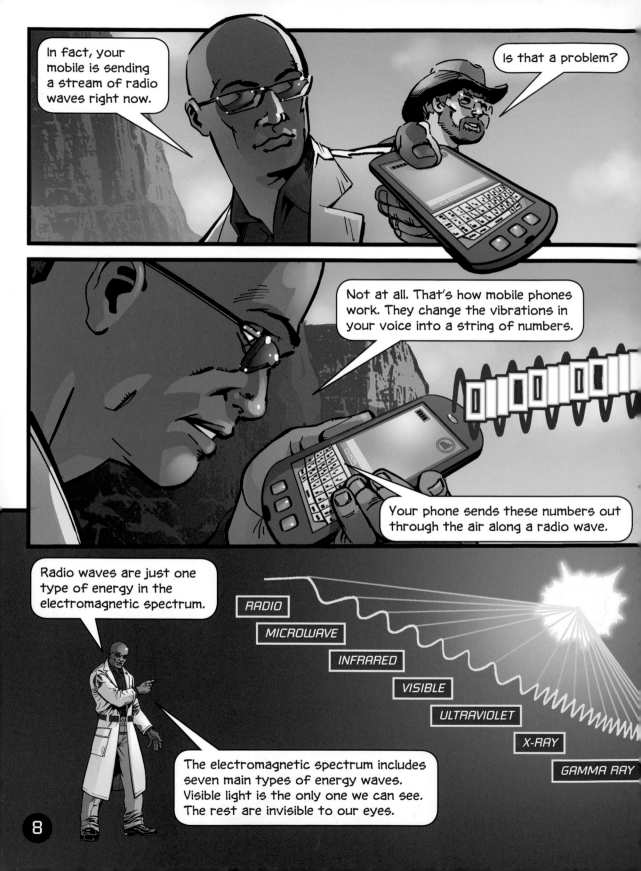

Within the spectrum, energy waves are grouped together by their frequencies. Frequency is the number of times a wave moves up and down per second.

Frequency is measured with a unit called hertz. If a wave moves up and down 20 times in a second, we call that 20 hertz.

ONE SECOND

Radio waves are on the slow end of the spectrum. Their frequencies range from 50 to 1,000 million hertz.

That still sounds fast.

While we can't see radio waves, we can create and tune into them. Mobile phones, TVs, radios and walkie-talkies all use this amazing technology.

Super Fast
Radio waves may have a slow frequency, but they travel at the speed of light. Light travels at 300,000 kilometres (180,000 miles) a second. That's fast enough to circle Earth seven times in one second.

9

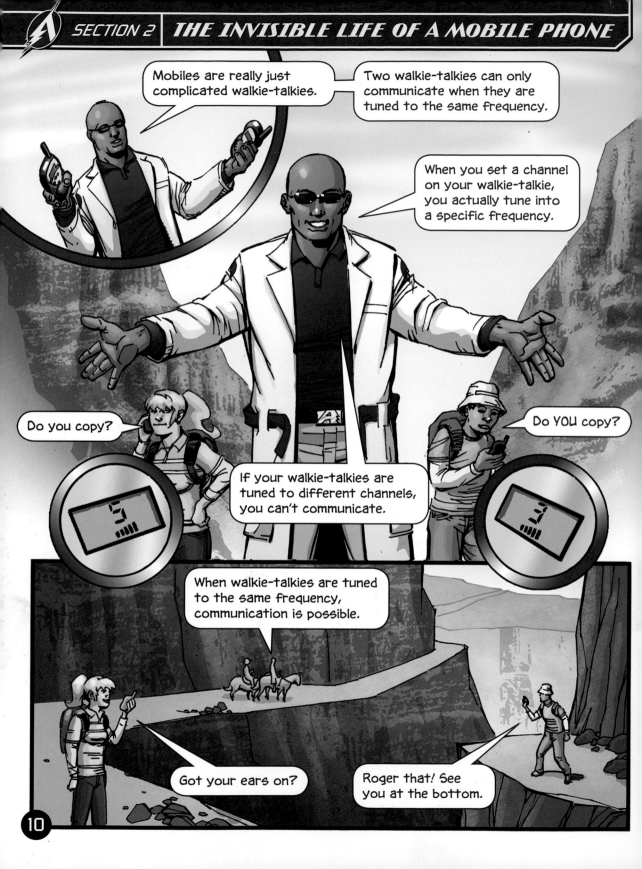

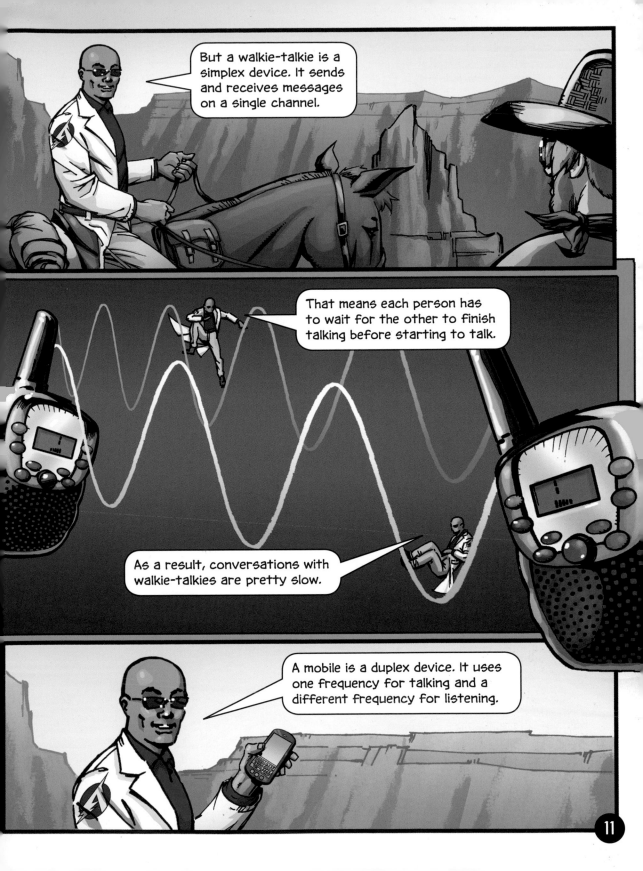

Two frequencies make it easier and faster to have a conversation.
Walkie-talkies have to be pretty close together to work. But mobile phones can connect across the globe. Do they use stronger radio waves?
Actually they don't. Mobile phones don't send signals directly to each other. They relay signals across long distances using mobile phone masts.

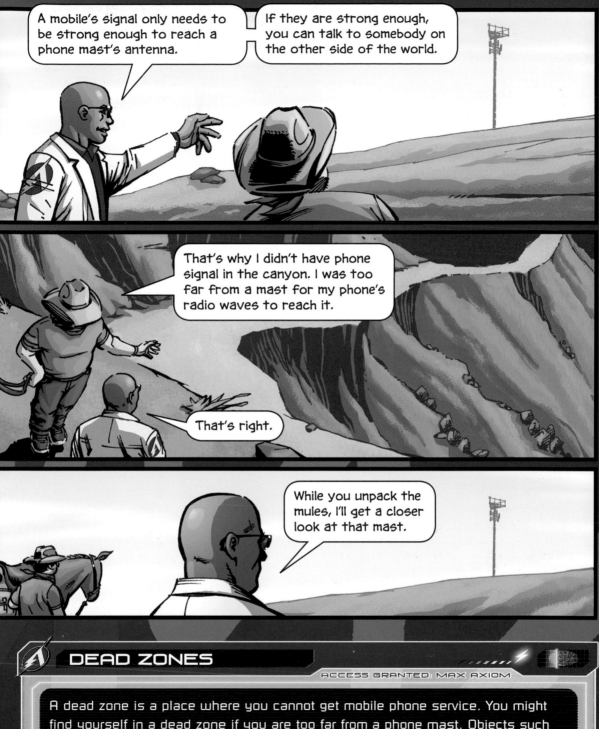

A mobile's signal only needs to be strong enough to reach a phone mast's antenna.

If they are strong enough, you can talk to somebody on the other side of the world.

That's why I didn't have phone signal in the canyon. I was too far from a mast for my phone's radio waves to reach it.

That's right.

While you unpack the mules, I'll get a closer look at that mast.

DEAD ZONES

ACCESS GRANTED: MAX AXIOM

A dead zone is a place where you cannot get mobile phone service. You might find yourself in a dead zone if you are too far from a phone mast. Objects such as mountains or tall buildings can block your signal to cause a dead zone. If you travel into a dead zone while using your phone, the communication will suddenly end. This situation is called a dropped call.

Remote areas have only a few phone masts because there are fewer people. But a city needs a lot more phone masts for the large number of mobile users.

Phone masts all over the city pick up radio waves from mobiles. Here, take a look.

As you can see, phone masts are harder to spot in cities. They usually aren't placed on top of towers.

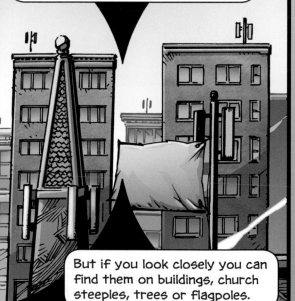

But if you look closely you can find them on buildings, church steeples, trees or flagpoles.

Thanks, Clyde! I'm off to see these phone masts close up.

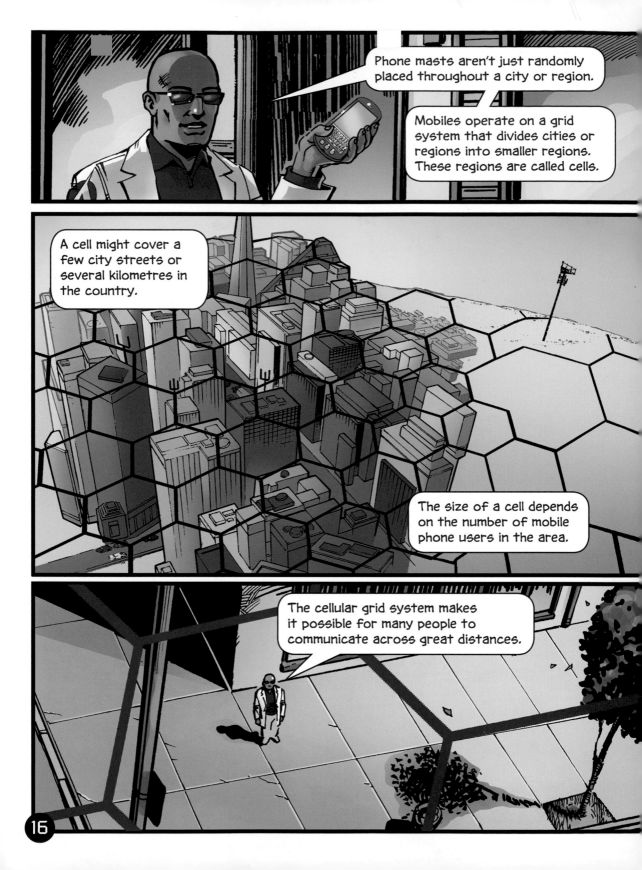

A phone mast inside each cell picks up signals from the mobiles within it.

Each cell is assigned a certain range of frequencies. Nearby cells use a different range of frequencies. But cells that aren't near each other can use the same frequencies.

Both of these callers are using the same frequencies to make separate calls. But because they are in different cells, their calls don't interfere with each other.

Lots of people are using the same frequencies at the same time right here in this city.

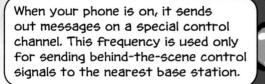

When your phone is on, it sends out messages on a special control channel. This frequency is used only for sending behind-the-scene control signals to the nearest base station.

As you travel with your mobile phone, different base stations track your location with these signals.

Your mobile phone company knows who you are and where you are because of these signals.

The electronic serial number (ESN) identifies your phone.

The mobile identification number (MIN) is your phone number.

The system identification number (SID) identifies the company that carries your phone service.

Your phone sends out these three numbers as it goes from cell to cell. They tell your phone company where you are and how many minutes you talk on your phone each month.

BILL

MINUTES USED

The control channel signals allow you to make calls. They also help locate you when someone is trying to call you.

ROAMING

Even if you travel in areas where your mobile phone company doesn't operate, other companies will carry your phone calls. But they sometimes charge you extra money to do it. This charge is for what phone companies call "roaming".

Now that we know how a mobile phone works, I better try calling Maria again.

Good idea.

All right! I have mobile service again. We must be within range of that base station.

Your phone is probably already sending out signals.

Even more amazing is all the work my phone does once I hit this button.

111-555-3214

MORE ABOUT
MOBILE PHONES

Satellite phones are another type of mobile phone. Instead of using phone masts to carry signals, they beam signals to a satellite high above the Earth. One satellite can do the work of thousands of mobile phone masts. Satellite phones are bulky and expensive today. But they may replace mobile phones someday.

Are mobile phones hazardous to your health? Electromagnetic radiation is produced by the waves used to send mobile phone messages. This radiation affects electrical activity in the brain. Some researchers suspect, but have yet to prove, that this radiation can cause cancer in the ears and brain.

The first successful mobile phone was invented by Motorola in 1973. Early mobile phones were neither small nor cheap. They were the size of a brick and sold for nearly £2,500!

New ways to use a mobile phone are constantly being engineered. Most mobile phone users can access the internet and take pictures with their phones. Engineers are now working on air writing. This technology will allow people to write words in the air with their phone. The words will then show up on the mobile phone's screen.

The touchscreen on a mobile phone is an amazing technology. Some touchscreens respond to the electrical currents in your finger. Others detect the location of your touch by noticing the interruption your finger causes in sound waves or visible light.

CRITICAL THINKING QUESTIONS

1. What type of energy waves do mobile phones use to make calls? Compare the characteristics of these waves to other types of energy waves in the electromagnetic spectrum.

2. Why does Max display colour-coded cellular grids on page 17? Explain how these illustrations help you understand the way frequencies are used in an area's mobile phone grid.

3. What three codes does a mobile phone always transmit when it is turned on? Explain why these codes are important to mobile phone companies.

MORE ABOUT

SUPER SCIENTIST

Real name: Maxwell J. Axiom
Hometown: Seattle, USA
Height: 1.85m   Weight: 87kg
Eyes: Brown   Hair: None

Super capabilities: Super intelligence; able to shrink to the size of an atom; sunglasses give x-ray vision; lab coat allows for travel through time and space.

Origin: Since birth, Max Axiom seemed destined for greatness. His mother, a marine biologist, taught her son about the mysteries of the sea. His father, a nuclear physicist and volunteer park ranger, schooled Max on the wonders of earth and sky.

One day on a wilderness hike, a megacharged lightning bolt struck Max with blinding fury. When he awoke, Max discovered a newfound energy and set out to learn as much about science as possible. He travelled the globe earning degrees in every aspect of the field. Upon his return, he was ready to share his knowledge and new identity with the world. He had become Max Axiom, Super Scientist.

 GLOSSARY

antenna (an-TEN-uh) – a wire or dish that sends or receives radio waves

duplex (DEW-pleks) – having two parts

electromagnetic spectrum (i-lek-troh-mag-NET-ic SPEK-truhm) – the wide range of energy given off by the Sun

engineer (en-juh-NEER) – someone trained to design and build machines, vehicles, bridges, roads or other structures

frequency (FREE-kwuhn-see) – the number of sound waves that pass a location in a certain amount of time

grid (GRID) – a pattern of evenly spaced, or parallel, lines that cross

hertz (HURTS) – a unit for measuring the frequency of vibrations and waves; one hertz equals one wave per second

radiation (ray-dee-AY-shuhn) – rays of energy given off by certain elements

radio wave (RAY-dee-oh WAYV) – a type of electromagnetic wave; electromagnetic waves are caused by electricity and magnetism

region (REE-juhn) – a large area

rural (RUR-uhl) – of the countryside; away from cities and towns

satellite (SAT-uh-lite) – a spacecraft used to send signals and information from one place to another

simplex (SIM-pleks) – having one part

Find Out More

Cell Phones (Let's Explore Science), Don McLeese, Rourke Publishing, 2010

Did You Invent the Phone All Alone, Alexander Graham Bell? (Scholastic Science Supergiants), Melvin and Gilda Berger, Scholastic, 2007

How Do Cell Phones Work? (Science in the Real World), Richard Hantula, Chelsea House Publishers, 2009

Zoom It: Invent New Machines that Move (Invent It), Tammy Enz, Fact Finders, 2012

Websites

www.bbc.co.uk/newsbeat/21630454

Be careful with your mobile phone! They can get lost and stolen easily. Here's some information about how to keep them safe!

www.cellphonesafety.org

This website talks about possible risks behind using a mobile phone.

www.childline.org.uk/explore/onlinesafety/pages/mobilesafety.aspx

Sometimes bullies can contact you on your mobile phone. Don't worry; this website has useful information that might help.